U0111778

大展好書　好書大展
品嘗好書　冠群可期

大展好書　好書大展
品嘗好書・冠群可期

少林傳統功夫漢英對照系列　❽

Shaolin Traditional Kungfu Series Books　❽

燕青拳

YanQing Boxing

耿 軍 著

Written by Geng Jun

大展出版社有限公司

作者簡介

　　耿軍（法號釋德君），1968 年 11 月出生於河南省孟州市，係少林寺三十一世皈依弟子。中國武術七段、全國十佳武術教練員、中國少林武術研究會副秘書長、焦作市政協十屆常委、濟南軍區特警部隊特邀武功總教練、洛陽師範學院客座教授、英才教育集團董事長。1989 年創辦孟州少林武術院、2001 年創辦英才雙語學校。先後獲得河南省優秀青年新聞人物、全國優秀武術教育家等榮譽稱號。

　　1983 年拜在少林寺住持素喜法師和著名武僧素法大師門下學藝，成爲大師的關門弟子，後經素法大師引薦，又隨螳螂拳一代宗師李占元、金剛力功于憲華等大師學藝。在中國鄭州國際少林武術節、全國武林精英大賽、全國武術演武大會等比賽中 6 次獲得少林武術冠軍；在中華傳統武術精粹大賽中獲得了象徵少林武術最高榮譽的「達摩杯」一座。他主講示範的 36 集《少林傳統功夫》教學片已由人民體育音像出版社出版發行。他曾多次率團出訪海外，在國際武術界享有較高聲譽。

　　他創辦的孟州少林武術院，現已發展成爲豫北地區最大的以學習文化爲主、以武術爲辦學特色的封閉式、寄宿制學校，是中國十大武術教育基地之一。

Brief Introduction to the Author

Geng Jun〔also named Shidejun in Buddhism〕, born in Mengzhou City of Henan Province, November 1968, is a Bud -dhist disciple of the 31st generation, the 7th section of Chinese Wu shu, national "Shijia" Wu shu coach, Vice Secretary General of China Shaolin Wu shu Research Society, standing committee member of 10th Political Consultative Conference of Jiaozuo City, invited General Kungfu Coach of special police of Jinan Military District, visiting professor of Luoyang Normal University, and Board Chairman of Yingcai Education Group. In 1989, he estab -lished Mengzhou Shaolin Wu shu Institute; in 2001, he estab -lished Yingcai Bilingual School · He has been successively awarded honorable titles of "Excellent Youth News Celebrity of Henan Province" "State Excellent Wu shu Educationalist" etc.

In 1983, he learned Wu shu from Suxi Rabbi, the Abbot of Shaolin Temple, and Grandmaster Sufa, a famous Wu shu monk, and became the last disciple of the

Grandmaster. Then recom – mended by Grandmaster Sufa, he learned Wu shu from masters such as Li Zhanyuan, great master of mantis boxing, and Yu Xianhua who specializes in Jingangli gong. He won the Shaolin Wu shu champion for 6 times in China Zhengzhou International Wu shu Festival, National Competition of Wu lin Elites, National Wu shu Performance Conference, etc. and one "Damo Trophy" that symbolizes the highest honor of Shaolin Wu shu in Chinese Traditional Wu shu Succinct Competition. 36 volumes teaching VCD of Shaolin Traditional Wu shu has been published and is – sued by People's Sports Audio Visual Publishing House. He has led delegations to visit overseas for many times, enjoying high reputation in the martial art circle of the world.

Mengzhou Shaolin Wu shu Institute, established by him, has developed into the largest enclosed type boarding school of Yubei (north of Henan Province) area, which takes knowledge as primary and Wu shu as distinctiveness, also one of China's top ten Wu shu education bases.

序　言

中華武術源遠流長，門類繁多。

少林武術源自嵩山少林寺，因寺齊名，是我國拳系中著名的流派之一。少林寺自北魏太和十九年建寺以來，已有一千五百多年的歷史。而少林武術也決不是哪一人哪一僧所獨創，它是歷代僧俗歷經漫長的生活歷程，根據生活所需逐步豐富完善而成。

據少林寺志記載許多少林僧人在出家之前就精通武術或慕少林之名而來或迫於生計或看破紅塵等諸多原因削髮爲僧投奔少林，少林寺歷來倡武，並經常派武僧下山，雲遊四方尋師學藝。還請武林高手到寺，如宋朝的福居禪師曾邀集十八家武林名家到寺切磋技藝，推動了少林武術的發展，使少林武術得諸家之長。

本書作者自幼習武，師承素喜、素法和螳螂拳李占元等多位名家，當年如饑似渴在少林寺研習功夫，曾多次在國內外大賽中獲獎。創辦的孟州少林武術院亦是全國著名的武術院校之一，他示範主講的 36 集《少林傳統功夫》教學 VCD 已由人民體育音像出版社發行。

本套叢書的三十多個少林傳統套路和實戰技法是少

林武術的主要內容，部分還是作者獨到心得，很值得一讀，該書還採用漢英文對照，使外國愛好者無語言障礙，爲少林武術走向世界做出了自己的貢獻，亦是可喜可賀之事。

張耀庭題
甲申秋月

Preface

Chinese Wushu is originated from ancient time and has a long history, it has various styles.

Shaolin Wushu named from the Shaolin Temple of Songshan Mountain, it is one of the famous styles in the Chinese boxing genre. Shaolin temple has more than 1500 years of history since its establishment in the 19th year of North Wei Taihe Dynasty. No one genre of Shaolin Wushu is created solely by any person or monk, but completed gradually by Buddhist monks and common people from generation to generation through long–lasting living course according to the requirements of life. As recording of Record of Shaolin Temple, many Shaolin Buddhist monks had already got a mastery of Wushu before they became a Buddhist monk, they came to Shaolin for tonsure to be a Buddhist monk due to many reasons such as admiring for the name of Shaolin, or by force of life or seeing through thevanity of life. The Shaolin Temple always promotes Wushu and frequently appoints Wushu Buddhist monks to go down the mountain to roam around for searching masters and learning Wushu from them. It also invites

Wushu experts to come to the temple, such as Buddhist monk Fuju of Song Dynasty, it once invited Wushu famous exports of 18 schools to come to the temple to make skill interchange, which promoted the development of Shaolin Wushu and made it absorb advantages of all other schools.

The author learned from many famous exports such as Suxi, Sufa and Li Zhanyuan of Mantis Boxing, he studied Chinese boxing eagerly in Shaolin Temple, and got lots of awards both at home and abroad, he also set up the Mengzhou Shaolin Wushu Institute, which is one of the most famous Wushu institutes around China. He makes demonstration and teaching in the 36 volumes teaching VCD of Shaolin Traditional Wushu, which have been published by Peoples sports Audio Visual publishing house.

There are more than 30 traditional Shaolin routines and practical techniques in this series of books, which are the main content of Shaolin Wushu, and part of which is the original things learned by the author, it is worthy of reading. The series books adopt Chinese and English versions, make foreign fans have no language barrier, and make contribution to Shaolin Wushu going to the world, which is delighting and congratulating thing.

Titled by Zhang Yaoting

目　錄
Contents

目
錄

說　明

（一）為了表述清楚，以圖像和文字對動作作了分解說明，練習時應力求連貫銜接。

（二）在文字說明中，除特別說明外，不論先寫或後寫身體的某一部分，各運動部位都要求協調活動、連貫銜接，切勿先後割裂。

（三）動作方向轉變以人體為準，標明前後左右。

（四）圖上的線條是表明這一動作到下一動作經過的線路及部位。左手、左腳及左轉均為虛線（┈┈►）；右手、右腳及右轉均為實線（──►）。

Instructions

(ⅰ) In order to explain clearly figures and words are used to describe the actions in multi steps. Try to keep coherent when exercising.

(ⅱ) In the word instruction, unless special instruction, each action part of the body shall act harmoniously and join coherently no matter it is written first or last, please do not separate the actions.

(ⅲ) The action direction shall be turned taking body as standard, which is marked with front, back, left or right.

(ⅳ) The line in the figure shows the route and position from this action to the next action. The left hand, left foot and turn left are all showed in broken line (┈┈►) ; the right hand, right foot and turn right are all showed in real line (──►) .

基本步型與基本手型
Basic stances and Basic hand forms

圖 1

圖 2

圖 3

圖 4

圖 5

圖 6

燕青拳

圖 7

圖 8

圖 9

圖 10

圖 11

圖 12

基本步型與基本手型

圖 13

圖 14

圖 15

圖 16

圖 17

圖 18

圖 19

圖 20

圖 21

基本步型

少林武術中常見的步型有：弓步、馬步、仆步、虛步、歇步、坐盤步、丁步、併步、七星步、跪步、高虛步、翹腳步 12 種。

弓步：俗稱弓箭步。兩腿前後站立，兩腳相距本人腳長的 4～5 倍；前腿屈至大腿接近水平，腳尖微內扣不超過 5°；後腿伸膝挺直，腳掌內扣 45°。（圖 1）

馬步：俗稱騎馬步。兩腳開立，相距本人腳長的 3～3.5 倍，兩腳尖朝前；屈膝下蹲大腿接近水平，膝蓋與兩腳尖上下成一條線。（圖 2）

仆步：俗稱單叉，一腿屈膝全蹲，大腿貼緊小腿，膝微外展，另一腿直伸平仆接近地面，腳掌扣緊與小腿成 90°夾角。（圖 3）

虛步：又稱寒雞步。兩腳前後站立，前後相距本人腳長的 2 倍；重心移至後腿，後腿屈膝下蹲至大腿接近水平，腳掌外擺 45°；前腿腳尖點地，兩膝相距 10 公分。（圖 4）

歇步：兩腿左右交叉，靠近全蹲；前腳全腳掌著地，腳尖外展，後腳腳前掌著地，臀部微坐於後腿小腿上。（圖 5）

坐盤步：在歇步的形狀下，坐於地上，後腿的大小腿外側和腳背均著地。（圖 6）

　　丁步：兩腿併立，屈膝下蹲，大腿接近水平，一腳尖點地靠近另一腳內側腳窩處。（圖7）

　　併步：兩腿併立，屈膝下蹲，大腿接近水平。（圖8）

　　七星步：七星步是少林七星拳和大洪拳中獨有的步型。一腳內側腳窩內扣於另一腳腳尖，兩腿屈膝下蹲，接近水平。（圖9）

　　跪步：又稱小蹬山步。兩腳前後站立，相距本人腳長的2.5倍，前腿屈膝下蹲，後腿下跪，接近地面，後腳腳跟離地。（圖10）

　　高虛步：又稱高點步。兩腳前後站立，重心後移，後腿腳尖外擺45°，前腿腳尖點地，兩腳尖相距一腳距離。（圖11）

　　翹腳步：在七星螳螂拳中又稱七星步，兩腿前後站立，相距本人腳長的1.5倍，後腳尖外擺45°，屈膝下蹲，前腿直伸，腳跟著地，腳尖微內扣。（圖12）

基本手型

　　少林武術中常見的手型有拳、掌、鉤3種。

　　拳：

　　分為平拳和透心拳。

　　平拳：平拳是武術中較普遍的一種拳型，又稱方拳。四指屈向手心握緊，拇指橫屈扣緊食指。（圖

13）

　　透心拳：此拳主要用於打擊心窩處，故名。四指併攏捲握，中指突出拳面，拇指扣緊抵壓中指梢節處。（圖14）

　　掌：

　　分為柳葉掌、八字掌、虎爪掌、鷹爪掌、鉗指掌。

　　柳葉掌：四指併立，拇指內扣。（圖15）

　　八字掌：四指併立，拇指張開。（圖16）

　　虎爪掌：五指分開，彎曲如鉤，形同虎爪。（圖17）

　　鷹爪掌：又稱鎖喉手，拇指內扣，小指和無名指彎曲扣於掌心處，食指和中指分開內扣。（圖18）

　　鉗指掌：五指分開，掌心內含。（圖19）

　　鉤：

　　分為鉤手和螳螂鉤。

　　鉤手：屈腕，五指自然內合，指尖相攏。此鉤使用較廣，武術中提到的鉤均為此鉤。（圖20）

　　螳螂鉤：又稱螳螂爪，屈腕成腕部上凸，無名指、小指屈指內握，食指、中指內扣，拇指梢端按貼於食指中節。（圖21）

Basic stances

Usual stances in Shaolin Wushu are: bow stance, horse stance, crouch stance, empty stance, rest stance, cross–legged sitting, T –stance, feet –together stance, seven –star stance, kneel stance, high empty stance, and toes –raising stance, these twelve kinds.

Bow stance: commonly named bow –and –arrow stance. Two feet stand in tandem, the distance between two feet is about four or five times of length of one´s foot; the front leg bends to the extent of the thigh nearly horizontal with toes slightly turned inward by less than 5°; the back leg stretches straight with the sole turned inward by 45°. (Figure 1)

Horse stance: commonly named riding step. two feet stand apart, the distance between two feet is 3~3.5 times of length of one´s foot, with tiptoes turned forward; bend knees to squat downward, with thighs nearly horizontal, knees and two tiptoes in line. (Figure 2)

Crouch stance: commonly named single split. Bend the knee of one leg and squat entirely with thigh very close to lower leg and knee outspread slightly; straighten the other leg and crouch horizontally close to floor, keep the sole turned inward and forming an included angle of 90° with lower leg. (Figure 3)

Empty stance: also named cold–chicken stance. Two feet stand in tandem, the distance between two feet is 2 times of length of one´s foot; transfer the barycenter to back leg, bend the knee of the back leg and squat downward to the extent of the thigh nearly horizontal, with the sole turned outward by 45°; keep the tiptoe of front leg on the ground, with distance between two knees of 10cm. (Figure 4)

Rest stance: cross the two legs at left and right, keep them close and entirely squat; keep the whole sole of the front foot on the ground with tiptoes turned outward, the front sole of the back foot on the ground, and buttocks slightly seated on the lower leg of the back leg. (Figure 5)

Cross – legged sitting: in the posture of rest stance, sit on the ground, with the outer sides of the thigh and lower leg of the back leg and instep on the ground. (Figure 6)

T – stance: two legs stand with feet together, bend knees and squat to the extent of the thighs nearly horizontal, with one tiptoe on the ground and close to inner side of the fossa of the other foot. (Figure 7)

Feet – together stance: two legs stand with feet together, bend knees and squat to the extent of the thigh nearly horizontal. (Figure 8)

Seven – star stance: Seven – star step is a unique step form in Shaolin Seven – star Boxing and Major Flood Boxing. Keep the inner side of the fossa of one foot turned inward onto tiptoe of the other foot, bend two knees and squat nearly horizontal. (Figure 9)

Kneel stance: also named small mountaineering stance. Two feet stand in tandem, the distance between two feet is 2.5

times of length of one´s foot, bend knee of the front leg and squat, kneel the back leg close to the floor, with the heel of back foot off the floor. (Figure 10)

High empty stance: also named high point stance. Two feet stand in tandem. Transfer the barycenter backward, turn the tiptoe of the back leg outward by 45°, with tiptoe of front leg on the ground, and the distance between two tiptoes is length of one foot. (Figure 11)

Toes −raising stance: also named seven −star stance in Seven −star Mantis Boxing. Two legs stand in tandem, and the distance between two legs is 1.5 times of length of one´s foot. Keep the tiptoe of back leg turned outward by 45°, bend knees and squat, straighten the front leg with heel on the ground and tiptoe turned inward slightly. (Figure 12)

Basic hand forms

Usual hand forms in Shaolin Wushu are: fist, palm and hook, these three kinds.

Fist: classified into straight fist and heart−penetrating fist.

Flat fist: a rather common fist form in Wushu, also named square fist. Hold the four fingers tightly toward the palm, and horizontally bend the thumb to button up the fore finger. (Figure 13)

Heart −penetrating fist: mainly used for striking the heart part. Put four fingers together and coil −hold them, the middle finger thrusts out the striking surface of the fist, the thumb

buttons up and presses the end and joint of the middle finger.
(Figure 14)

Palm: classified into willow leaf palm, splay palm, tiger´s
claw palm, eagle´s claw palm, fingers clamping palm.

Willow leaf palm: palm with four fingers up and thumb
turned inward. (Figure 15)

Eight–shape palm: palm with four fingers up and thumb
splay. (Figure 16)

Tiger´s claw palm: palm with five fingers apart, bent as
hook and like tiger´s claw. (Figure 17)

Eagle´s claw palm: also named throat locking hand, with
the thumb turned inward, the little finger and middle finger
turned onto palm, fore finger and middle finger apart and turned
inward. (Figure 18)

Fingers clamp palm: palm with five fingers apart and palm
drawn in. (Figure 19)

Hook: classified into hook hand and mantis hook.

Hook hand: bend the wrist, five fingers drawn in naturally
with fingertips together. This hook is used in wide range, the
hook mentioned in Wushu refers to this. (Figure 20)

Mantis hook: also named mantis´ claw, bend wrist into
wrist bulge upward, the ring finger and little finger bend to hold
inward, with fore finger and fore middle finger turned inward
and end of thumb pressed on the middle joint of the fore finger.
(Figure 21)

燕青拳套路簡介

Brief Introduction to the Routine YanQing Boxing

燕青拳起源於唐末，傳至宋代時由盧俊義在少林寺加以發展而成。盧俊義收燕青為徒，後燕青廣泛傳授此拳，故稱燕青拳。

本套路共由53個動作組成。動作輕靈敏捷，靈活多變，講究腰腿功，功架端正，發力充足，是少林寺傳統的優秀套路之一。

YanQing Boxing, as one of excellent routines of traditional Shaolin Wushu, was originated at the end of Tang Dynasty, and developed by Lu Junyi at Shaolin Temple in Song Dynasty. Lu Junyi taught this boxing skill to Yanqing, his apprentice. Then YanQing taught it broadly, thus, it was named YanQing Boxing. This routine consists of 53 postures. Its actions are light and agile, flexible and changeful, with decent frame and enough force exert, emphasizing the skills of the waist and legs.

燕青拳套路動作名稱
Action Names of Routine
YanQing Boxing

第一段 Section One

1. 預備勢　Preparatory posture
2. 虛步亮掌　Flash palm in empty stance
3. 迎面腳　Head-on foot
4. 弓步推掌　Push palm in bow stance
5. 虛步抄拳　Uppercut with fist in empty stance
6. 馬步劈砸　Hack and pound in horse stance
7. 翻身弓步雙推掌　Turn over, push palms in bow stance
8. 彈腿橫推掌　Snap kick and push transverse palm
9. 倒步劈拳　Step back and hack with fist
10. 虛步挎肘　Carry elbow in empty stance
11. 轉身馬步架打　Turn body, parry and punch in horse stance
12. 虛步挎肘　Carry elbow in empty stance
13. 弓步撩陰拳　Upper-cut croth in bow stance
14. 虛步抄拳　Upper-cut with fist in empty stance
15. 馬步劈砸　Hack and pound in horse stance

16. 翻身弓步雙推掌　Turn over, push palms in bow stance

第二段　Section Two

17. 彈腿橫推掌　Snap kick and push transverse palm
18. 後踹腿　Backward heel kick
19. 摟手弓步沖拳　Brush hand and thrust fist in bow stance
20. 馬步劈砸　Hack and pound in horse stance
21. 震腳彈腿沖拳　Stamp foot, snap kick and thrust fist
22. 馬步架打　Parry and punch in horse stance
23. 弓步架打　Parry and punch in bow stance
24. 沖天炮　Sky cannon
25. 糊眼窩心肘　Elbow toward the heart for guarding the eyes
26. 挑打插捶　Pick strike and insert hammer
27. 翻身弓步雙推掌　Turn over, push palms in bow stance

第三段　Section Three

28. 彈腿橫推掌　Snap kick and push transverse palm
29. 弓步一拳　Punch in bow stance
30. 震腳上步一掌　Stamp foot, step forward and push

燕青拳套路動作名稱

palm

31. 掄臂仆步砸　Swing arms, pound in crouch stance

32. 蘇秦背劍　Su Qin carries the sword behind his body

33. 快馬加鞭　Whip the rapid horse

34. 仆步劈掌　Hack with palm in crouch stance

35. 分掌踹腿　Separate palms and kick with heel

36. 摟手弓步沖拳　Brush hand and thrust fist in bow stance

37. 撩陰腳　Upper–cut croth with foot

38. 雙手甩鏢　Two hands throw darts

39. 二起腳　Jumping kick twice

40. 獨立鎖喉　Lock throat in single–leg stance

41. 仆步穿掌　Thread palm in crouch stance

42. 摟手弓步沖拳　Brush hand and thrust fist in bow stance

第四段　Section Four

43. 左擒右蹬踢　Left capture and right stamp

44. 摟手弓步沖拳　Brush hand and thrust fist in bow stance

45. 馬步劈砸　Hack and pound in horse stance

46. 搖身觀陣　Sway body to witness a battle

47. 旋風腳　Whirlwind foot

48. 馬步架打　Parry and punch in horse stance

49. 猛虎出洞　Fierce tiger comes out of the cave
50. 虛步亮掌　Flash palm in empty stance
51. 上步一掌　Step forward and push palm
52. 虛步穿喉掌　Thread palm in empty stance
53. 二起腳　Jumping kick twice
54. 虛步打虎　Beat tiger in empty stance
55. 收勢　Closing form

燕青拳套路動作名稱

燕青拳套路動作圖解
Action Illustrtion of Routine
YanQing Boxing

圖 1

第一段　Section One

1. 預備勢　Preparatory posture

（1）兩腳自然站立；兩手自然下垂，成立正勢；目視前方。（圖1）

（1）Standnaturally with feet together; the hands drop naturally, stand at attention. Eyes look forward.〔Figure 1〕

圖 2

(2) 上動不停。開左步，與肩同寬；兩掌變拳，與肩同寬，雙拳抱於腰際；目視左方。（圖 2）

要點：挺胸塌腰，頭正頸直。抱拳、開步同時進行，迅速俐落。

(2) Keep the above action, the left foot steps apart from the right one, at shoulder–width. Change the two palms in to fists at shoulder –width, hold the two fists on the waist. Eyes look leftward. (Figure 2)

Key points: lift the chest and bow downward, with head being correctitude and neck straight, holding fists on hips and put the feet apart shall be done simultaneously, quickly and without further ado.

圖3

2. 虛步亮掌　Flash palm in empty stance

（1）接上勢。後撤右步，成左弓步；右手自腰間向後、向前繞環；左拳仍抱於腰際；目視右掌。（圖3）

（1）Follow the above posture, draw back the right foot into left bow stance, swing the right hand backward and forward from the chest and the waist, still hold the left fist on the waist. Eyes look at the right palm.（Figure 3）

圖4

(2)上動不停。左手經右臂向前穿出；右手屈肘回收於左胸前；左弓步不變。（圖4）

(2) Keep the above action, thread the left hand forward through the right arm, bend the right elbow to draw back the right hand to the front of the left chest, keep in bow stance. (Figure 4)

圖5

(3) 上動不停。收左腳扣腿；右掌向右、向後甩
擺；左掌向上擺架；目視右掌。（圖5）

(3) Keep the above action, draw back the left foot to press
behind right knee, and swing the right palm rightward and
backward. Swing and parry the left palm upward. Eyes look at
the right palm. 〔Figure 5〕

圖 6

　　(4)上動不停。左腳落地成虛步；左手變鉤手向後勾摟；右手向頭右上方擺架，掌心向上，掌指向左；目視左方。（圖6）

　　要點：各動作力求輕靈流暢，連貫協調。

　　(4) Keep the above action, the left foot falls to the ground into empty stance, change the left hand into hook hand and grab it backward, swing and parry the right hand and place it above the right part of the head, keep the palm upward and the fingers leftward. Eyes look leftward.（Figure 6）

　　Key points: every action shall be agile and fluent, coherent and harmony.

圖 7

3. 迎面腳　Head－on foot

（1）接上勢。左腳向前上步，重心前移，身體上提，上體動作不變；目視前方。（圖 7）

(1) Follow the above posture, the left foot steps for－ward, move the barycenter forward and raise the body. Keep the action of the upper body. Eyes look forward.﹝Figure 7﹞

燕青拳套路動作圖解

圖 8

(2)上動不停。右腳向前上方踢腿，上體姿勢仍不
變；目視右腳尖。（圖 8）

(2) Keep the above action, kick the right leg upward ahead.
Still keep the action of the upper body. Eyes look at the right
tiptoe.〔Figure 8〕

圖 9

(3) 上動不停。落右腳成馬步；左臂姿勢不變；右掌置於胸前，掌心向上，掌指向左；目視右方。（圖9）

要點：踢腿要短促有力，快速收回。

(3) Keep the above action, the right foot falls into horse stance, keep the posture of the left arm, and place the right palm in the front of the chest. Keep the palm upward and the fingers leftward. Eyes look rightward.〔Figure 9〕

Key points: kicking shall be transient and forceful, draw the leg back quickly.

圖 10

4. 弓步推掌 Push palm in bow stance

接上勢。身體右轉 90°成右弓步；右掌向前推出，掌心向前，掌指向上；目視前方。（圖 10）

要點：轉身與推掌要連貫協調，動作快速有力。

Follow the above posture, turn the body 90° to the right. Push the palm forward with the fingers up.Eyes look forward. （Figure 10）

Key points: turning the body and pushing the palm shall be coherent and consistent; the action shall be quick and forceful.

圖 11

5. 虛步抄拳
Uppercut with fist in empty stance

接上勢。上右腳成左虛步；同時，左手變拳，屈臂向前上抄出；右手附於左前臂上；目視左拳。（圖11）

Follow the above posture, the right foot steps forward into left empty stance. At the same time, change the left hand into fist, bend the arm to uppercut with the fist, keep the right hand close to the left forearm. Eyes look at the left fist. 〔Figure 11〕

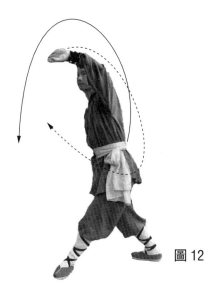

圖12

6. 馬步劈砸

Hack and pound in horse stance

⑴接上勢。左腳上一步，腳尖外擺，身體上提；同時，左手從胸前向上、向左翻掌繞環；目視左前方。（圖12）

⑴ Follow the above posture, the left foot takes a step forward with toes turned outward, raise the body. At the same time, swing the left hand from the front of the chest while turning over the left palm upward and leftward. Eyes look leftward ahead.〔Figure 12〕

圖 13

（2）上動不停。上右腳，左轉體 90°成馬步；右手變拳繞環下砸；左手附於右前臂內側；目視右拳。（圖13）

要點：劈砸要腰肩發力，勁力迅猛。

（2）Keep the above action, the right foot steps forward, turn the body 90° to the left into horse stance. Change the right hand into fist and swing it downward for pounding, keep the left hand close to the inner side of the right forearm. Eyes look at the right fist.〔Figure 13〕

Key points: when hacking and pounding, twist the waist and snap the shoulder to send strength that shall　be swift.

圖 14

7. 翻身弓步雙推掌

Turn over, push palms in bow stance

(1) 接上勢。雙腳蹬地起跳；雙手隨起跳自左向右擺動。（圖 14）

(1) Follow the above posture, the feet jump up form the ground, swinging the hands left to right.（Figure 14）

圖 15

（2）上動不停。右腳落地，同時左轉體 180°；雙手
繼續掄臂。（圖 15）

(2) Keep the above action, the right foot lands to the ground,
at the same time, turn the body 180° to the left, continuously
swinging　the arms.（Figure 15）

圖 16

(3) 上動不停。左腳落地成馬步；雙手掄臂收於兩腰際；目視前方。（圖 16）

(3) Keep the above action, the left foot lands to the ground into horse stance, draw the two hands back on the waist. Eyes look forward.〔Figure 16〕

圖 17

　　⑷上動不停。重心移於左腳成左弓步；同時，雙掌向前推出，掌心向前，掌指向上；目視前方。（圖17）

　　要點：推掌轉體要與擰腰發力協調一致。

⑷ Keep the above action, move the barycenter to the left foot into right bow stance. At the same time, push the two palms forward, keep the palm forward and the fingers upward. Eyes look forward.（Figure 17）

Key points: Pushing palms with body turn shall be consistent with twisting waist to apply force.

圖 18

8. 彈腿橫推掌
Snap kick and push transverse palm

(1) 接上勢。左掌收於胸前，右手外抓變拳；弓步不變；目視右拳。（圖 18）

(1) Follow the above posture, draw back the left palm to the front of the chest, clench the right hand into fist. Keep in bow stance. Eyes look at the right fist. (Figure 18)

圖 19

　　(2)上動不停。右拳收回腰間；同時，重心移於左
腿，右腿向正前上方彈踢；橫推左掌，掌心向外，掌
指向右；目視左掌。（圖19）

　　要點：踢腿與推掌要協調一致，同步完成。

　　(2) Keep the above action, draw back the right fist on the
waist. At the same time, shift the barycenter to the left leg, the
right leg kicks frontal upward ahead. Horizontally push the left
palm with the palm outward and the fingers rightward. Eyes look
at the left palm.〔Figure 19〕

　　Key points: kicking and pushing the palm shall be harmony
and consistent, done simultaneously.

圖 20

9. 倒步劈拳
Step back and hack with fist

(1)接上勢。落右腳，跳提左腳；同時，右拳上提至頭部右側，左手掄至左前下方；目視左前下方。（圖 20）

(1) Follow the above posture, the right foot lands to the ground, jump up to lift the left foot. At the same time, raise the right fist to the right side of the head, swing the left hand left downward ahead. Eyes look left downward ahead. 〔Figure 20〕

圖 21

(2)上動不停。左腳在身後落步成左弓步;同時,
右拳下砸;左手附於右前臂內側。(圖 21)

要點:下砸要順肩發力,乾脆俐落。

(2) Keep the above action, the left foot lands behind the
body into left bow stance. At the same time, pound the right fist
downward and keep the left hand close to the inner side of the
right forearm.〔Figure 21〕

Key points: when pounding downward, send the shoulders
to apply force without further ado.

燕青拳套路動作圖解

圖 22

10. 虛步挎肘 Carry elbow in empty stance

（1）接上勢。左轉體 90°成馬步；左掌變拳，向左屈
肘撥擋，拳心向右後方；右拳回抱腰間；目視左拳。
（圖 22）

(1) Follow the above posture, change the left hand into fist,
turn the body 90° to the left into horse－riding, stance, change
the left palm into fist and bend the left elbow to block aside with
the fist－palm right backward, draw back the right fist and hold it
on the waist. Eyes look at the left fist.（Figure 22）

圖 23

　　(2)上動不停。左拳繼續向外撥擋回抱腰間；右拳
經胸前向右屈肘撥擋，拳心向左後方；目視右拳。
（圖 23）

　　(2) Keep the above action, parry the left fist forward
continuously, draw it back and hold on the waist, bend the right
elbow and parry it rightward through the front of the chest with
the fist–palm left backward. Eyes look at the right fist.（Figure
23）

圖 24

(3) 上動不停。上右腳變右虛步；右拳繼續向外撥擋向後環繞經腰間，屈臂向前、向上抄拳，拳心向後；上體略下蹲前傾；目視右拳。（圖 24）

要點：抱臂要擰腰抖肩，動作連貫，發力迅猛。

(3) Keep the above action, the right foot steps forward into right empty stance. Parry outward continuously with the right fist and circle it backward through the waist, bend the arm and uppercut forward ahead with the fist—palm backward, squat and slant the body slightly. Eyes look at the right fist. (Figure 24)

Key points: when holding the arm, twist the waist and snap the shoulders to send strength that shall be swift, the action shall be coherent.

圖 25

11. 轉身馬步架打
Turn body, parry and punch in horse stance

　接上勢。身體右轉 180°，步隨身轉，震右腳，上左步成馬步；右手掄臂向上架拳；左拳向左沖擊，與肩同高，拳心向下；目視左拳。（圖 25）

　要點：震腳有力，馬步穩固，兩手動作配合協調。

燕青拳套路動作圖解

Follow the above posture, turn the body 180° to the right, move with body turn and stamp the right foot; the left feet steps forward and left ward into horse stance, keep the right hand holding the arm and parry the fist upward, punch the left fist leftward with the fist–plam down, at shoulder height. Eyes look at the left fist. (Figure 25)

Key points: stamping foot shall be forceful, horse stance shall be steady, the cooperation of the two hands shall be harmonious.

圖 26

12. 虛步挎肘　Carry elbow in empty stance

(1)接上勢。身體上提；右拳經胸前向外屈肘撥擋，拳心向左後方；左拳回抱於腰間；馬步不變；目視前方。（圖 26）

(1) Follow the above posture, raise the body and parry the right fist outward through the front of the chest with the fist – palm left backward, draw back the left fist and hold it on the waist, keep in horse stance. Eyes look forward. 〔Figure 26〕

圖 27

(2) 上動不停。右拳繼續向後擺動；左拳經胸前向
外撥擋，拳心向右後方；馬步不變。（圖 27）

(2) Keep the above action, swing the right fist backward
continuously, parry the left fist outward through the front of the
chest with the fist–palm right backward, keep in horse stance.
〔Figure 27〕

圖 28

(3) 上動不停。左拳繼續向外撥擋，回抱腰間；同時，上右步成右虛步，身體略下蹲；右拳經腰間向前上方抄出，拳心向後；目視右拳。（圖 28）

(3) Keep the above action, continuously parry the left fist outward, draw it back and hold on the waist, at the same time, the right foot steps forward into right empty stance, slightly squat the body, lift the right fist upward ahead through the waist with the fist-palm backward. Eyes look at the right fist.〔Figure 28〕

圖 29

13. 弓步撩陰拳
Upper-cut croth in bow stance

(1) 接上勢。右腳向左橫跨一步成馬步；右拳屈肘置於左胸前，拳心向上；目視右方。（圖 29）

(1) Follow the above posture, the right foot strides a step leftward into horse stance, bend the right elbow and place the right fist in front of the left chest with the fist-palm up. Eyes look rightward. (Figure 29)

圖 30

(2)上動不停。身體右轉成右弓步；右拳經腹前向上、向前撩出，拳心向下，拳眼向左，與肩同平；左拳仍抱於腰間；目視右拳。（圖 30）

(2) Keep the above action, turn the body to the right into right bow stance. Uppercut with the right fist upward ahead through the front of the abdomen, keep the fist－palm downward and the fist－hole leftward, at shoulder level. Still hold the left fist on the waist. Eyes look at the right fist.〔Figure 30〕

圖 31

14. 虛步抄拳
Upper-cut with fist in empty stance

接上勢。上左腳成左虛步；左拳屈臂向上抄出；
右手搭於左前臂上，身體後坐；目視前方。（圖 31）

Follow the above posture, The left foot steps forward into
left empty stance, bend the arm to uppercut with left fist, place
the right hand on the left forearm. Draw the body backward.
Eyes look forward.（Figure 31）

圖 32

15. 馬步劈砸
Hack and pound in horse stance

⑴接上勢。起身，左腳外擺踏實；右手變拳向後擺動；左拳變掌向上擺架。（圖 32）

(1) Follow the above posture, swing the left foot outward and steps firmly, raise the body, change the right hand into fist and swing the fist backward, change the left fist into palm, swing and parry it upward.（Figure 32）

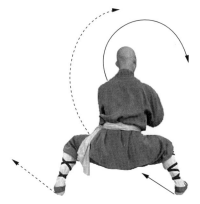

圖 33

(2) 上動不停。上右腳成馬步；同時，右拳從後向前揚起，屈臂向下砸；同時，左手變掌外翻，與右臂相擊；目視右拳。（圖 33）

(2) Keep the above action, the right foot steps forward into horse stance, at the same time, swing the right fist backward to forward, bend the arm and pound it downward. At the same time, change the left hand into palm and turn it outward to counterpunch the right arm. Eyes look at the right fist.（Figure 33）

圖 34

16. 翻身弓步雙推掌

Turn over, push palms in bow stance

（1）接上勢。雙腳蹬地騰空跳換步；雙掌同時從胸前自左向右摟撥。（圖 34）

（1）Follow the above posture, the feet jump up from the ground, at the same time grab the two palms left to right from the front of the chest.〔Figure 34〕

圖 35

(2) 上動不停。右腿落地；左掌摟於左前方，右手
置於身後；目視左前方。（圖 35）

(2) Keep the above action, the right leg lands to the ground,
grab the left palm leftward ahead and place the right hand behind
the body. Eyes look leftward ahead.（Figure 35）

圖 36

(3) 上動不停。兩手抱臂收於腰間；同時，左腳落地成馬步；目視左方。（圖 36）。

(3) Keep the above action, bend both arms to draw hands back on the waist. At the same time, the left foot lands to the ground into horse stance. Eyes look leftward. 〔 Figure 36 〕

圖 37

(4) 上動不停。重心前移成左弓步；雙掌向前推出，臂與肩平，兩掌心向前，掌指向上；目視前方。（圖 37）

(4) Keep the above action, shift the barycenter forward into left bow stance, push forward with the two palms, keep the arm at shoulder level, the two palms forward and the fingers up. Eyes look forward.〔Figure 37〕

燕青拳

圖 38

第二段　Section Two

17. 彈腿橫推掌
Snap kick and push transverse palm

(1)接上勢。左掌回收附於右上臂上方，掌心向下；右手外抓變拳，拳心向上；左弓步不變；目視右拳。（圖 38）

(1) Follow the above posture, draw back the left palm and keep it close to the right upper arm with the palm downward. Clench the right hand outward into fist with the fist-palm up, keep in left bow stance. Eyes look at the right fist.（Figure 38）

圖 39

(2)上動不停。右拳收於腰間；同時，彈踢右腿；
橫推左掌，掌心斜向下，掌指向右，與肩同高；目視
左掌。（圖 39）

(2) Keep the above action, draw back the right fist on the
waist. At the same time, kick with the right foot, horizontally
push the left palm, keep the palm downward aslant and the
fingers rightward, at shoulder height. Eyes look at the left palm.
（Figure 39）

圖 40

18. 後踹腿　Backward heel kick

（1）接上勢。右腿屈膝收回；右拳與左掌在胸前相擊；目視前下方。（圖 40）

(1) Follow the above posture, bend the right knee to draw back the right leg, striking the right fist to the left palm in front of the chest. Eyes look downward ahead.〔Figure 40〕

圖 41

　(2)上動不停。身體右轉 90°，右腿向右後方踹腿，高過頭頂；左手抓右拳抱於腹部；目視右腳。（圖 41 ）

　　要點：轉身要輕靈，踹腿要有力，連貫協調。

　(2)Keep the above action, turn the body 90° to the right, kick the right leg right backward, higher than the head top. The left hand grabs the right fist and hold together in front of the abdomen. Eyes look at the right foot.〔Figure 41〕

　　Key points: turning the body shall be agile; kicking shall be forceful, coherent and harmony.

圖 42

19. 摟手弓步沖拳
Brush hand and thrust fist in bow stance

　　接上勢。向右落右腳成右弓步，同時，身體右轉90°；右手外摟變拳收回腰間；左拳向前沖出，拳心向下，拳眼向右，與肩同高；目視前方。（圖 42）

Follow the above posture, the right foot falls rightward into right bow stance. At the same time, turn the body 90° to the right, grab the right hand outward and change it into fist, draw the fist back on the waist, punch the left fist forward, keep the fist－plam down and the fist－hole rightward, at shoulder height. Eyes look forward. ﹝Figure 42﹞

燕青拳套路動作圖解

圖 43

20. 馬步劈砸
Hack and pound in horse stance

接上勢。身體左轉成馬步；左拳變掌，向上、向外繞環；右拳掄臂下砸，左掌與右臂相擊；目視右拳。（圖 43）

要點：劈砸要速猛，以肩帶臂發力。

Follow the above posture, turn the body to the left into horse–riding step, change the left fist into palm and swing it upward and outward, hold the right fist on the arm and pounding it downward, strike the left palm to the right arm. Eyes look at the right fist.（Figure 43）

Key points: hacking and pounding shall be swift, the shoulders bring the arms to send strength.

圖 44

21.震腳彈腿沖拳
Stamp foot, snap kick and thrust fist

（1）接上勢。身體左轉 90°；左掌外摟變拳；右拳抱於腰間；同時，上右腳，併步震腳。（圖 44）

（1）Follow the above posture, turn the body 90° to the left, grab the left palm outward into fist, hold the right fist on the waist, at the same time, the right foot steps forward, put the feet together and stamp with the right foot.（Figure 44）

燕青拳套路動作圖解

圖 45

(2)上動不停。左拳收回腰間；右拳向前沖出；同時，向前彈踢左腿。（圖 45）

要點：震腳明顯而有力，兩腳並齊，各動作要協調連貫。

(2) Keep the above action, draw back the left fist and hold it on the waist, punch the right fist forward. At the same time, kick the left foot forward.（Figure 45）

Key points: stamp the foot apparently and forcefully, put the feet together, every action shall be harmony and coherent.

圖 46

22. 馬步架打
Parry and punch in horse stance

接上勢。落左腳成馬步；右手掄臂架拳於頭頂右上方；左拳沖出，拳心向下，與肩同高；目視左方。（圖 46）

Follow the above posture, the left foot falls into horse – riding stance, the right hand hold the arm and parry the fist right upward above the head, punch the left fist with the fist –palm down, at shoulder level. Eyes look leftward.〔Figure 46〕

圖 47

23. 弓步架打
Parry and punch in bow stance

⑴接上勢。左拳屈臂下壓，拳心向上；右拳收於腰間；目視左拳。（圖 47）

(1) Follow the above posture, bend the left fist and press it downward with the fist–palm up, draw back the right fist on the waist. Eyes look at the left fist. 〔Figure 47〕

圖 48

(2)上動不停。身體左轉 90°成左弓步；同時，左拳上架於頭上方；右拳前沖，與肩同平，拳心向下；目視前方。（圖 48）

(2) Keep the above action, turn the body 90° to the left into left bow stance. At the same time, lift the left fist above the head, punch the right fist forward, at shoulder level with the fist–palm down. Eyes look forward. 〔 Figure 48 〕

圖 49

24. 沖天炮　Sky cannon

接上勢。右拳外翻，屈臂下掛，向前上方沖出，隨即收回；左拳上架姿勢不變；目視前方。（圖 49）

要點：右拳沖出與收回要有反彈力，速猛連貫完成。

Follow the above posture, turn the right fist outward and bend the arm to hang the fist downward, punch it upward ahead, then draw it back. Keep the posture of lifting up the left fist. Eyes look forward.（Figure 49）

Key points: punching the right fist and drawing it back shall be done through rebounding force, and completed swiftly and coherently.

圖 50

25. 糊眼窩心肘
Elbow toward the heart for guarding the eyes

(1) 接上勢。提右腿，重心移於左腿；右拳回收腰間；同時，左拳變掌，經右臂外側向左前方推出；目視左掌。（圖 50，圖 50 附圖）

燕青拳套路動作圖解

圖 50 附圖

(1) Follow the above posture, raise the right leg and move the barycenter onto the left one; draw back the right fist back on the waist, at the same time, change the left fist into palm, and push it leftward ahead through the outer side of the right arm. Eyes look at the left palm.（Figure 50, Attached figure 50）

圖 51

(2)上動不停。落右腳成馬步；右臂屈肘橫擊；左手擊拍右臂；目視前方。（圖 51，圖 51 附圖）

要點：橫擊要控腰抖肩，發力迅猛，動作連貫，協調一致。

圖 51 附圖

(2) Keep the above action, the right foot lands into horse stance, bend the right elbow to horizontally punch, the left hand strikes on the right arm. Eyes look forward. (Figure 51, Attached figure 51)

Key points: Horizontal punch shall control the waist and snap the shoulder, release force swiftly, the action, shall be coherent and consistent.

圖 52

26. 挑打插捶
Pick strike and insert hammer

(1) 接上勢。抬左腳，右腳蹬地跳起，左腳落地，右腳提膝；右拳屈臂上挑；左手迎擊右臂。（圖 52、圖 52 附圖）

圖 52 附圖

(1) Follow the above posture, raise the left foot, the right one jumps up from the ground while the left one lands to the ground, raise the right knee. Bend the right arm and thrust the right fist upward, the left hand counterpunches the right arm. （Figure 52, Attached figure 52 ）

圖 53

(2)上動不停。落右腳成右虛步，身體下蹲，微斜於左側；右拳向前插擊；左掌迎擊右拳面；目視前方。（圖 53、圖 53 附圖）

圖 53 附圖

(2) Keep the above action, the right foot lands into right empty stance, the body squats and slightly slants at the left side. Insert the right fist to pound forward, the left palm counterpunches the right fist–place. Eyes look forward. (Figure 53, Attached figure 53)

圖 54

27. 翻身弓步雙推掌
Turn over, push palms in bow stance

⑴接上勢。雙腳騰空；雙手同時自左向右摟撥。
（圖 54）

⑴ Follow the above posture, the feet jump up, at the same time, grab the hands leftward to rightward． （Figure 54）

圖 55

(2) 上動不停。右腳落地；左手摟撥於左前方；右
手擺於身後。（圖 55）

(2) Keep the above action, the right foot lands to the ground,
grab the left hand left forward, swing the right hand behind the
body.（Figure 55）

圖 56

（3）上動不停。左腳落地成馬步；雙手變掌，收於腰間；目視左方。（圖 56）

(3) Keep the above action, the left foot lands into horse stance. Change the two hands into palms and draw them back on the waist. Eyes look leftward.（Figure 56）

圖 57

(4) 上動不停。身體左轉 90°成左弓步；雙掌向前推出，掌心向前，掌指向上；目視前方。（圖 57）

要點：跳換步要輕靈，騰空要高，推掌要力達掌根。

(4) Keep the above action, turn the body 90° to the left into left bow stance, push the two palms forward, keep the palm forward and the fingers upward. Eyes look forward. (Figure 57)

Key points: jumping to change the step shall be agile, jumping up shall be high, and the strength for pushing the palms shall reach the palm-base.

圖 58

第三段　Section Three

28. 彈腿橫推掌
Snap kick and push transverse palm

⑴接上勢。左掌收於右臂肘窩處，右手外抓變拳，
拳心向上；左弓步不變。（圖 58）

(1) Follow the above posture, draw back the left palm to the
right cubital fossa, clench the right hand outward into fist with
the fist-palm up. Keep in the left bow stance.〔Figure 58〕

圖 59

(2)上動不停。右拳回抱於腰間；同時，向前彈踢右腿；橫推左掌，掌心向下，掌指向右；目視左掌。（圖 59）

(2) Keep the above action, draw back the right fist and hold it on the waist. At the same time, kick the right leg forward and horizontally push the left palm, keep the palm downward and the fingers rightward. Eyes look at the left palm. ﹝ Figure 59 ﹞

圖 60

29. 弓步一拳　Punch in bow stance

　　接上勢。落右腳成右弓步；左掌變拳收回腰間；右拳前沖，與肩同高，拳心向下，拳眼向左；目視前方。（圖 60）

Follow the above posture, the right foot falls into right bow step, draw back the left palm on the waist and change it into fist, punch the right fist forward, at shoulder level, keep the fist – palm down and the fist –hole leftward. Eyes look forward. （Figure 60）

燕青拳套路動作圖解

圖 61

30. 震腳上步一掌
Stamp foot, step forward and push palm

接上勢。震右腳；上左步成左弓步；右拳拉回腰
間；同時，左拳變掌前推，掌心向前，掌指向上；目
視前方。（圖 61）

Follow the above posture, stamp the right foot, the left foot
steps forward into left bow stance, draw back the right fist on the
waist. At the same time, push the left fist into palm forward,
keep the palm forward and the fingers upward. Eyes look
forward.〔Figure 61〕

圖 62

31. 掄臂仆步砸
Swing arms, pound in crouch stance

（1）接上勢。起身；左掌變拳，左拳向後；右拳向前擺動。（圖 62）

(1) Follow the above posture, raise the body, change the left palm into fist, swing the left fist backward and the right one forward.〔Figure 62〕

圖 63

(2)上動不停。身體右轉 180°；兩手繼續掄臂繞環。（圖 63）

(2) Keep the above action, turn the body 180° to the right, continuously swing the arms to circle the two hands.（Figure 63）

圖 64

(3)上動不停。身體下蹲，落為右仆步；右拳向右
腳方向下砸；左拳向後擺至頭部左上方；目視右拳。
（圖 64）

要點：掄臂要迅猛，下砸要有力，協調連貫。

(3) Keep the above action, squat the body, lower the right leg into right crouch stance; the right fist pounds towards the right foot, swing the left one backward and lift it above the left part of the head. Eyes look at the right fist. (Figure 64)

Key points: swinging the arms together shall be swift, pounding downward shall be forceful, coherent and consistent.

圖 65

32. 蘇秦背劍
Su Qin carries the sword behind his body

(1)接上勢。起身，身體右轉 90°成右弓步；兩拳變掌向前探出，掌心向下，掌指向前；目視前方。（圖 65）

(1) Follow the above posture, raise the body, turn the body 90° to the right into right bow stance, change the two fist into palms and stretch them forward, keep the palm downward and the fingers forward. Eyes look forward.（Figure 65）

圖 66

（2）上動不停。右掌屈肘挑掌立於胸前，掌心向左，掌指向上；同時，右腳收回成右虛步；左手後擺成鉤手；目視前方。（圖 66）

(2) Keep the above action, bend the right elbow and lift the palm to stand it in front of the chest, keep the palm leftward and the fingers up. At the same time, draw back the right foot into right empty stance, swing the left hand backward into hook hand. Eyes look forward.〔Figure 66〕

圖 67

33. 快馬加鞭 Whip the rapid horse

接上勢。右腿屈膝上提成左獨立勢；右掌變拳，
向右方下截，臂微屈；左鉤手置於身後不動；目視右
拳。（圖 67）

Follow the above posture, bend the right knee and raise it
into single−leg stance; change the right palm into fist and punch
the fist right downward slightly, keep the left hook hand static at
the bake of the body. Eyes look at the right fist.〔Figure 67〕

圖 68

34. 仆步劈掌
Hack with palm in crouch stance

(1) 接上勢。左腳蹬地跳起，同時身體右轉 180°；
雙臂揚起。（圖 68）

(1) Follow the above posture, the left foot jumps up from the
ground, at the same time, twist the waist and turn the body 180°
to the right. Lift the two hands.﹙Figure 68﹚

圖 69

(2)上動不停。雙腳落地成右仆步；雙掌在胸前交叉下劈，左掌在內，右掌在外；目視右掌。（圖 69、圖 69 附圖）

圖 69 附圖

(2) Keep the above action, the feet land to the ground into right crouch stance; cross the two palms in front of the chest and hack them downward. Keep the left palm inside and the right one outside. Eyes look at the right palm. (Figure 69, Attached figure 69)

圖 70

35. 分掌踹腿

Separate palms and kick with heel

（1）接上勢。起身，右腳後插；兩掌繞環交叉於胸前；目視左方。（圖 70、圖 70 附圖）

圖 70 附圖

(1) Follow the above posture, raise the body to insert the right foot, circle the two palms in front of the chest. Eyes look leftward. ﹝Figure 70, Attached figure 70﹞

圖 71

(2)上動不停。左腳向左上方踹出；同時，兩掌從胸前呈水平向兩側推出，掌心向外；目視左腳。（圖71）

(2) Keep the above action, kick upward right with the left foot left, at the same time, horizontally push the two palms to both sides of the body through the front of the chest with the palms outward. Eyes look at the left foot.（Figure 71）

圖 72

36. 摟手弓步沖拳
Brush hand and thrust fist in bow stance

接上勢。落左腳成左弓步；左手外摟變拳，收於
腰間；右拳向前沖出，拳心向下，拳眼向左，與肩同
高；目視右拳。（圖 72）

Follow the above posture, the left foot falls into left bow
stance; grab the left hand outward into fist and draw it back on
the waist, punch the right fist forward, keep the fist–palm down
and the fist–hole leftward, at shoulder level. Eyes look at the
right fist.（Figure 72）

圖 73

37. 撩陰腳　Uppercut croth with foot

接上勢。右拳回抱於腰間，兩拳心向上；右腳向前、向上彈踢；目視右腳尖。（圖 73）

要點：腳面繃直，力達腳尖。

Follow the above posture, draw back the right fist and hold it on the waist, keep the fist－palms of the two fists up, kick forward and upward with the right foot. Eyes look at the right tiptoe.〔Figure 73〕

Key points: stretch the instep straight with the strength reaching the tiptoe.

圖74

38. 雙手甩鏢　Two hands throw darts

(1) 接上勢。落右腳，身體右轉成交叉步，兩腿微屈；雙手下插，掌心向內；目視前方。（圖74）

(1) Follow the above posture, the right foot lands, turn the body to the right into cross stance, slightly bend the two legs. Punch the two hands downward with the palm inward. Eyes look forward.（Figure 74）

燕青拳

圖 75

（2）上動不停。兩腿直立；雙手經胸前向兩側甩出，與肩同高，掌心向上，掌指向外；目視左掌。（圖 75）

(2) Keep the above action, the two legs stand upright, throw the two hands to both sides of the body through the front of the chest, at shoulder level, keep the palm up and the fingers outward. Eyes look at the left palm.（Figure 75）

燕青拳套路動作圖解

圖 76

39. 二起腳 Jumping kick twice

(1) 接上勢。身體左轉；左手經右臂外側向前穿掌；右手回收置於左腋下。（圖 76）

(1) Follow the above posture, turn the body to the left, thread the left palm forward through the outer side of the right arm, place the right hand under the right axilla. (Figure 76)

圖 77

(2) 上動不停。抬左腳，右腳蹬地騰空向前、向上踢起；左掌變鉤手向後擺動；右掌拍擊右腳面；目視右腳。（圖 77）

(2) Keep the above action, raise the left foot, the right one jumps from the ground and kicks upward ahead, change the left hand into hook hand and swing it backward, the right palm slaps the right instep. Eyes look at the right foot.〔Figure 77〕

圖 78

40. 獨立鎖喉
Lock throat in single-leg stance

(1) 接上勢。雙腳下落成馬步；左鉤手變掌雙掌畫弧交叉置於胸前，左手在外，右手在內；目視右手。（圖 78）

(1) Follow the above posture, fall the twice raising foot into horse stance, change the left hook–hand into palm swing the two palms to draw a circle and cross them in front of the chest, keep the left hand outside and the right one inside. Eyes look at the right hand.（Figure 78）

圖 79

　(2)上動不停。左腳提膝，成右獨立勢；右手經左臂內側向右上探出鎖喉；左掌變拳抱於腰間；目視右手。（圖 79）

　(2) Keep the above action, raise the left knee into single‑leg stance, stretch the right hand rightward and upward through the inner side of the left arm to lock the throat, change the left palm into fist and hold it on the waist. Eyes look at the right hand.〔Figure 79〕

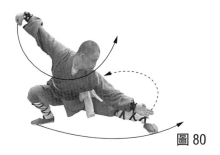

圖 80

41. 仆步穿掌　Thread palm in crouch stance

接上勢。屈膝下蹲，左腳向左鏟步平仆成左仆步；同時，右手變鉤手臂伸直；左拳變掌向左腳方向穿掌；目視左掌。（圖 80）

Follow the above posture, bend the knees to squat the body, shovel leftward with the outer edge of the left foot into left crouch stance. At the same time, change the right hand into hook hand with the arm straight, change the left fist into palm out towards the left foot. Eyes look at the left palm. (Figure 80)

圖 81

42. 摟手弓步沖拳
Brush hand and thrust fist in bow stance

接上勢。上右腿，身體左轉 180°成左弓步；同時，左手向前、向外摟抓變拳收於腰間；右手變拳，經腰間向右側沖出；目視右拳。（圖 81、圖 81 附圖）

圖 81 附圖

Follow the above posture, the right foot steps forward, turn the body 180° to the left into left bow stance. At the same time, grab the left hand outward ahead. Change the right hand into fist and punch it to the right side of the body through the waist. Eyes look at the right fist. ﹝Figure 81, Attached figure 81﹞

圖 82

第四段　Section Four

43. 左擒右蹬踢　Left capture and right stamp

（1）接上勢。雙手變掌，在胸前交叉，左手在內，右手在外，右掌從左臂上回拉至體後；插左步成交叉步；左掌向前橫推，掌指向右；目視左掌。（圖 82、圖 82 附圖）

圖 82 附圖

(1) Follow the above posture, change the two hands into palms and cross them in front of the chest with the left palm inside and the right one outside, draw back the right palm behind the body from the right arm, insert the left foot into cross stance, horizontally push the left palm forward with the fingers rightward. Eyes look at the left palm. (Figure 82, Attached figure 82)

圖 83

（2）上動不停。撤右腳成左弓步；同時，左掌變拳收於腰間；右掌向前、向下橫擊，掌指斜向下；目視右掌。（圖 83、圖 83 附圖）

燕青拳套路動作圖解

圖 83 附圖

(2) Keep the above action, the right foot steps backward into left bow stance. At the same time, change the left palm into fist and draw it back to the waist, horizontally punch the right palm downward ahead with the fingers downward aslant. Eyes look at the right palm. (Figure 83, Attached figure 83)

圖 84

44. 摟手弓步沖拳
Brush hand and thrust fist in bow stance

　　接上勢。身體右轉 90°成右弓步；同時，右手外摟變拳收於腰間；左拳向前沖出，高與肩平，拳心向下，拳眼向右；目視前方。（圖 84）

　　Follow the above posture, turn the body 90° to the right into right bow step. At the same time, grab the right hand outward into fist and draw it back on the waist, punch the left fist forward, at shoulder level, keep the fist−palm downward and the palm hole rightward. Eyes look forward.〔Figure 84〕

燕青拳套路動作圖解

圖 85

45. 馬步劈砸
Hack and pound in horse stance

　　接上勢。身體左轉 90°成馬步；同時，左拳回收掄臂下砸；左拳變掌與右臂相擊；目視左掌。（圖 85）

Follow the above posture, turn the body 90° to the left into horse stance. At the same time, draw back the left fist, change the right hand into fist and swing the arm to pound downward, change the left fist into palm and counterpunch the right arm. Eyes look at the left palm. (Figure 85)

圖 86

46. 搖身觀陣　Sway body to witness a battle

（1）接上勢。兩臂微屈，左掌變拳在胸前向裏抱臂搖格；右拳後擺；馬步不變。（圖 86）

（1）Follow the above posture, slightly bend the two arms, change the left palm into fist holds the arm inward in front of the chest, swing and parry with the left fist, swinging the right fist backward. Keep in horse stance.（Figure 86）

圖 87

　　(2) 上動不停。右臂在胸前繼續掄格，左拳後擺；
馬步不變。（圖 87）

　　(2) Keep the above action, swing to parry with the right arm
continuously, swing the left fist backward. Keep in horse stance.
（Figure 87）

圖88

（3）上動不停。收右腳成右虛步；同時，左拳擺架於頭左上方，拳心向右；右拳擺置於右後側；目視右前方。（圖88、圖88附圖）

要點：動作連貫，流暢。

燕青拳套路動作圖解

圖 88 附圖

(3) Keep the above action, draw back the right foot into right empty stance. At the same time, swing and lift the left fist above the left part of the head with the fist –centre rightward, swing and place the right fist at the right side behind the body. Eyes look rightward ahead. ﹝Figure 88, Attached figure 88﹞

Key points: the action shall be coherent and fluent.

圖 89

47. 旋風腳

Whirlwind foot

(1)接上勢。向右上步成馬步;左拳向下,右拳向上擺動;目視左手。(圖 89、圖 89 附圖)

圖 89 附圖

(1) Follow the above posture, the right foot steps rightward into horse stance, swing the left fist downward and the right one upward. Eyes look at the left hand. ﹝ Figure 89, Attached figure 89 ﹞

圖 90

(2)上動不停。左擰身騰空翻轉 360°做旋風腳；左手空中擊響右腳內側；目視右腳。（圖 90）

要點：轉身裏合腿要連貫迅捷，騰空要高，拍擊力要點準確，聲音要清脆。

(2) Keep the above action, twist the body, jump up and turn over 360° into whirlwind foot, the left hand lap the inner side of the right foot in the air with sound. Eyes look at the right foot. 〔Figure 90〕

Key points: swinging the leg inward with body turn shall be coherent and quick; jump high; the point of clapping force shall be accurate and the sound shall be clear.

燕青拳套路動作圖解

圖 91

48. 馬步架打
Parry and punch in horse stance

接上勢。雙腳落地成馬步；同時，左掌向左掄架
於頭頂上方；右拳向右沖出，拳心向下，拳眼向右，
高與肩平；目視右方。（圖 91）。

Follow the above posture, the feet falls to the ground into
horse stance. At the same time, swing the left palm above the
headtop, punch the right fist rightward, keep the fist –palm
downward and the fist –hole rightward, at shoulder level. Eyes
look rightward.〔Figure 91〕

圖 92

49. 猛虎出洞
Fierce tiger comes out of the cave

（1）接上勢。收右腳，併步震腳，身體右轉 180°，上左腳成馬步；同時，左掌為拳，雙拳回收於腰間；上體前傾；目視右前方。（圖 92）

(1) Follow the above posture, draw back the right foot to put the feet together, stamp the right foot, turn the body 180° to the right, the left foot steps forward into horse stance. At the same time, change the left palm into fist, swing the two fists on the waist. Slightly slant the body forward. Eyes look rightward ahead.〔Figure 92〕

燕青拳套路動作圖解

圖 93

(2) 上動不停。右腳提起扣於左膝後側，上身前伸；雙拳拳心相對，向前上方沖出；目視右前方。（圖 93）

(2) Keep the above action, raise the right foot and turn it inward onto the backside of the left knee, the upper body stretch forward. Punch the two fists upward ahead with the fist–palms opposite. Eyes look rightward ahead. ﹝Figure 93﹞

圖 94

50. 虛步亮掌　Flash palm in empty stance

（1）接上勢。落右步，上體直立；雙手變掌，右掌屈臂回抱；左掌經右臂內側向前穿掌；目視左手。（圖 94）

(1) Follow the above posture, the right foot lands, the body stands upright, change the two hands into palms and bend the arms to draw them back, thread the left palm forward through the inner side of the right arm. Eyes look at the left hand. （Figure 94）

圖 95

(2) 上動不停。左腳提膝扣於右膝後側；左掌擺架
於頭上方；右掌向右後方擺動；目視右手。（圖 95）

(2) Keep the above action, raise the left knee and turn the
left foot inward to the backside of the right knee, swing and
parry the left palm above the head and the right one right
backward. Eyes look at the right hand.（Figure 95）

圖 96

(3)上動不停。落左腳成虛步；同時，左掌採抓成
鉤，擺置於後方，鉤尖向上；右手擺架於頭上方，手
心向上，手指向左；目視左前方。（圖 96）

(3) Keep the above action, the left foot falls into empty
stance. At the same time, grab the left palm into hook hand,
swing and place it backside with the hook–tip up and the right
one above the head, keep the hand–palm up and the fingers
leftward. Eyes look leftward ahead.〔Figure 96〕

圖 97

51. 上步一掌　Step forward and push palm

(1)接上勢。左腳向左橫跨一步，成左馬步；右掌下落收至胸前下按；左掌前擺於腰間，掌心向上；目視右掌。（圖 97）

(1) Follow the above posture, the left foot strides a step leftward into left horse stance, the right palm falls; draw the right palm back to the front of the chest and press it downward; swing the left palm forward to the waist with the palm up. Eyes look at the right palm.（Figure 97）

圖 98

(2)上動不停。身體左轉成左弓步，左掌從右臂內側旋轉翻腕，然後向前推出，掌心向前，掌指向上；右掌收回腰間；目視前方。（圖 98）

(2) Keep the above action, turn the body 90° to left into bow stance, rotate the left palm and turn over the wrist from the inner side of the right arm, and then push it forward, keep the palm forward and the fingers upward; draw back the right palm to the waist, Eyes look forward.（Figure 98）

圖 99

52. 虛步穿喉掌　Thread palm in empty stance

接上勢。上右步成右虛步；左掌屈臂回收；右掌經左掌上向前穿出，掌心向上，掌指向前；目視前方。（圖 99）

要點：推掌要抖肩發力，與虛步要連貫協調完成。

Follow the above posture, the right foot steps forward into right empty stance, bend the left arm to draw back the left palm, thread the right palm forward through above the left palm, keep the palm up and the fingers forward. Eyes look forward. (Figure 99)

Key points: when pushing the palm, snap the shoulders to send trength, which shall be completed coherently and in harmony with changing into empty stance.

圖 100

53. 二起腳　Jumping kick twice

接上勢。左掌變鉤手平擺；左腳蹬地起跳，右腿屈膝向前、向上彈踢；右掌拍打右腳面；目視右腳。（圖 100）

Follow the above posture, change the left palm into hook hand and horizontally swing it, jump up by the left leg, lift the right leg and kick it upward ahead, the right palm slaps the right instep. Eyes look at the right foot.（Figure 100）

圖 101

54. 虛步打虎　Beat tiger in empty stance

⑴接上勢。身體左轉 90°後下蹲，左腳落地，右腳併步震腳；左鉤手變拳屈臂擺於頭頂左上方，拳心向右；右掌變拳隨即收回腰間；目視右方。（圖 101）

⑴ Follow the above posture, turn the body 90° to the left, and then squat the body, the left foot lands to the ground, put the right one together with it and stamp the right foot; bend the left arm and swing change the left hook – hand into fist above the left part of the head, keep the fist – palm rightward, then draw back change the right palm into fist and hold it on the waist. Eyes look rightward.（Figure 101）

圖 102

（2）上動不停。上左步，腳尖點地成左虛步；左拳收回腰間；右拳上架於頭頂右上方，拳心向前上方，拳眼向左；目視左前方。（圖 102）

（2）Keep the above action, the left foot steps forward with toes on ground into left empty stance, draw the left fist back and hold it on the waist, lift the right fist above the right part of the head, keep the fist－up up ahead and the fist－hole leftward. Eyes look leftward ahead.〔Figure 102〕

圖 103

55. 收勢　Closing form

（1）接上勢。收左腳，併步站立；同時，右拳收於
腰際；目視前方。（圖 103）

（1）Follow the above posture, draw back the left foot, put
the feet together and stands upright. At the same time, draw back
the right fist and hold it on the waist. Eyes look forward.
（Figure 103）

圖 104

(2)上動不停。兩手同時自然下垂至身體兩側，成立正勢；目視前方。（圖 104）

要點：平心靜氣，體態自然，精神內斂。

Keep the above action, the two hands simultaneously drop at both sides of the body, stand at attention. Eyes look forward. （Figure 104）

Key points: be calm in natural posture, collect the vital energy inward.

全套動作演示圖

Demonstration of All the Action

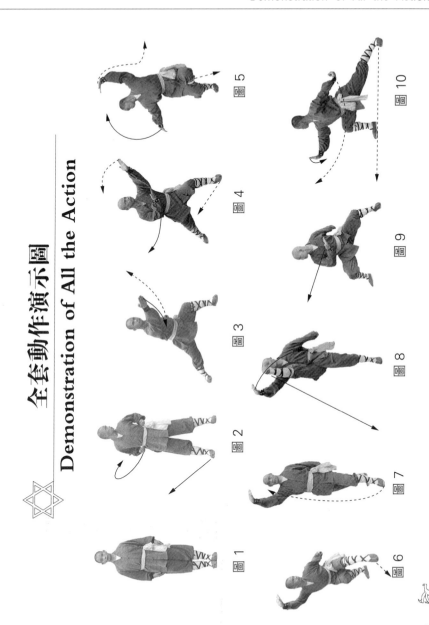

全套動作演示圖

燕青拳

圖 15

圖 20

圖 14

圖 19

圖 13

圖 18

圖 12

圖 17

圖 11

圖 16

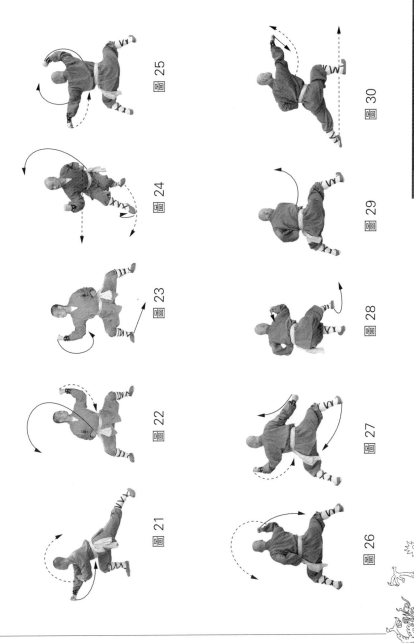

全套動作演示圖

圖 25　圖 24　圖 23　圖 22　圖 21

圖 30　圖 29　圖 28　圖 27　圖 26

燕青拳

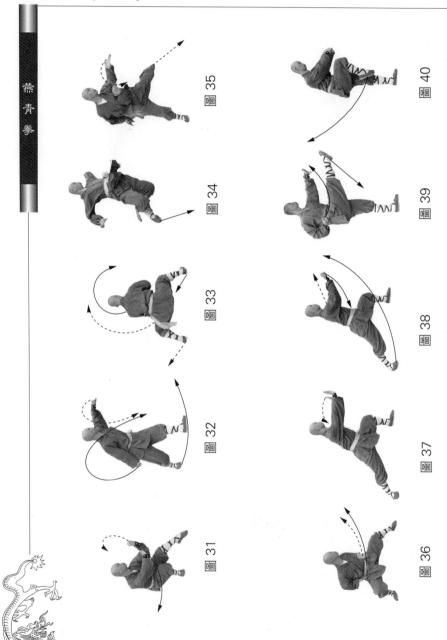

图35　图34　图33　图32　图31

图40　图39　图38　图37　图36

全套動作演示圖

圖 45

圖 44

圖 43

圖 42

圖 41

圖 50 附

圖 50

圖 49

圖 48

圖 47

圖 46

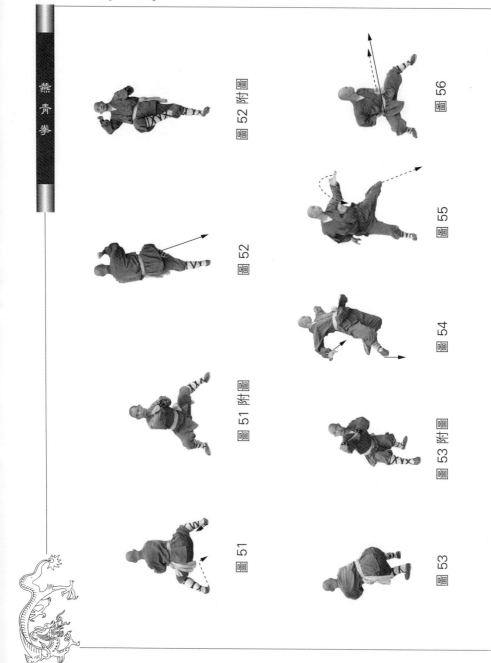

燕青拳

图 52 附图

图 52

图 56

图 55

图 54

图 51 附图

图 53 附图

图 51

图 53

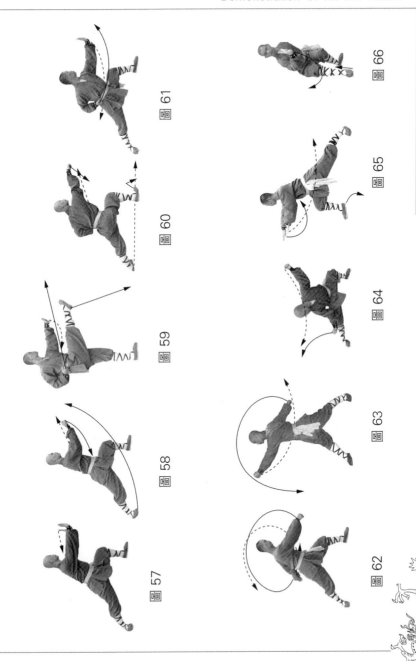

全套動作演示圖

圖 66

圖 65

圖 64

圖 63

圖 62

圖 61

圖 60

圖 59

圖 58

圖 57

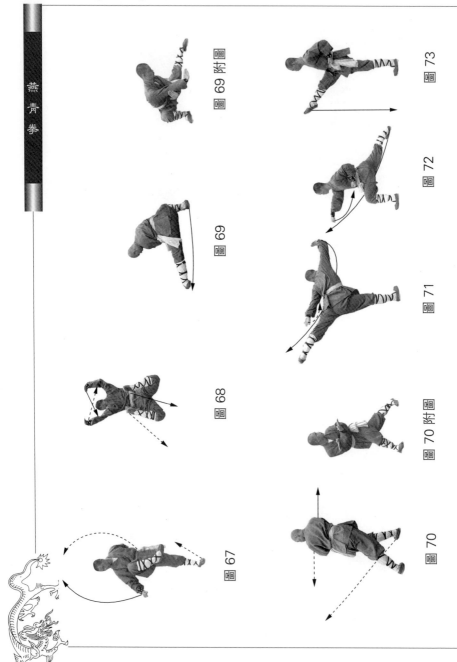

燕青拳

圖69附圖

圖73

圖72

圖69

圖71

圖68

圖70附圖

圖67

圖70

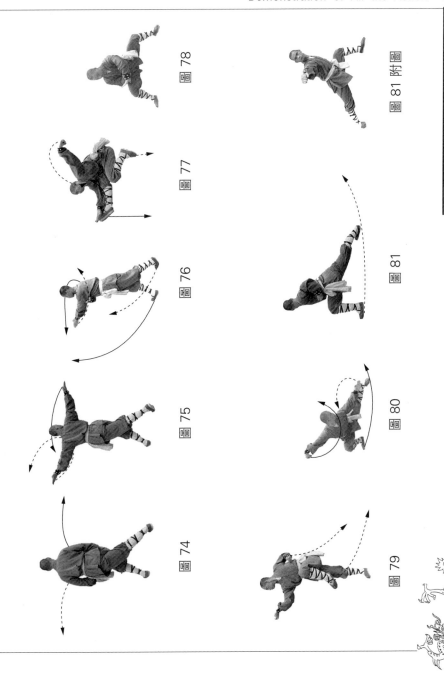

圖 78

圖 77

圖 76

圖 75

圖 74

圖 81 附

圖 81

圖 80

圖 79

全套動作演示圖

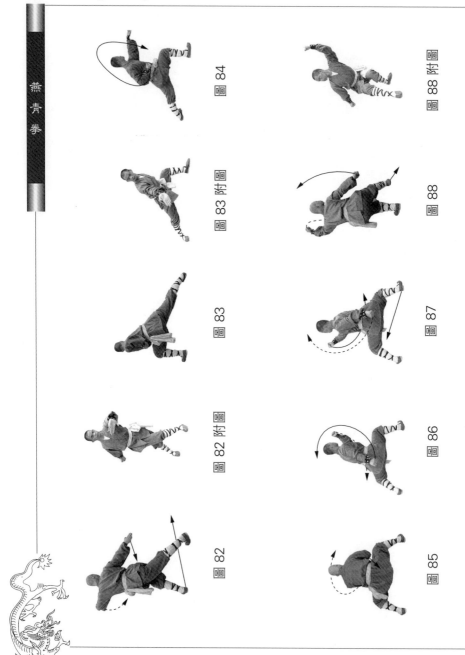

圖 84　　圖 88 附圖

圖 83 附圖　　圖 88

圖 83　　圖 87

圖 82 附圖　　圖 86

圖 82　　圖 85

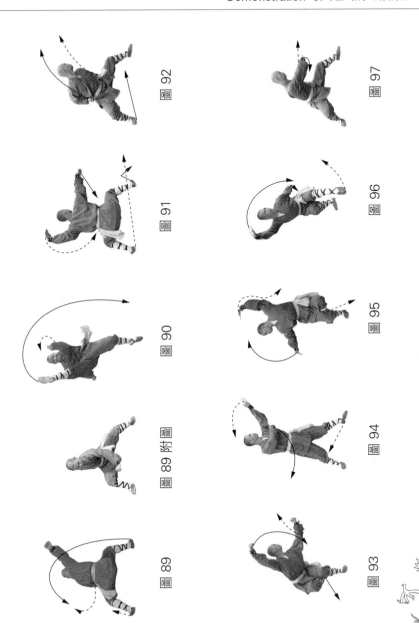

圖 92

圖 97

圖 91

圖 96

圖 90

圖 95

圖 89 附圖

圖 94

圖 89

圖 93

燕青拳

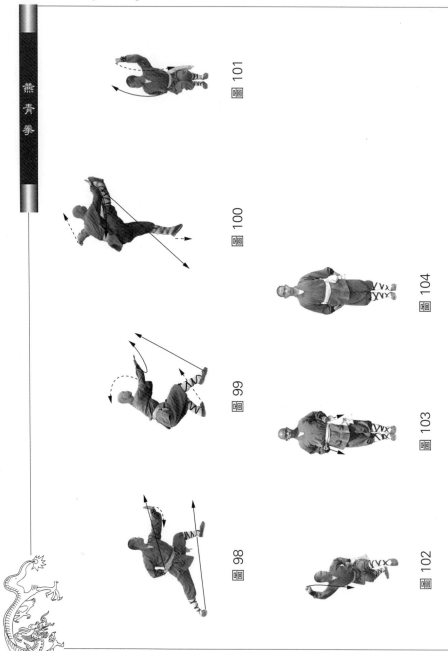

图 101

图 100

图 104

图 99

图 103

图 98

图 102

歡迎至本公司購買書籍

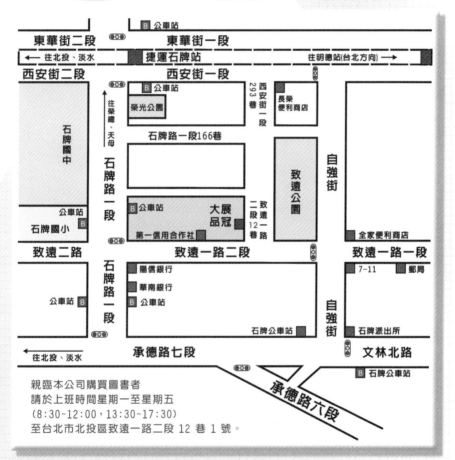

親臨本公司購買圖書者
請於上班時間星期一至星期五
(8:30~12:00，13:30~17:30)
至台北市北投區致遠一路二段 12 巷 1 號。

建議路線

1. 搭乘捷運‧公車

　　淡水線石牌站下車，由出口出來後，左轉(石牌捷運站僅一個出口)，沿著捷運高架往台北方向走(往明德站方向)，其街名為西安街，至西安街一段293巷進來(巷口有一公車站牌，站名為自強街口)，本公司位於致遠公園對面。搭公車者請於石牌站(石牌派出所)下車，走進自強街，遇致遠路口左轉，右手邊第一條巷子即為本社位置。

2. 自行開車或騎車

　　由承德路接石牌路，看到陽信銀行右轉，此條即為致遠一路二段，在遇到自強街(紅綠燈)前的巷子左轉，即可看到本公司招牌。

國家圖書館出版品預行編目資料

燕青拳＝YanQing Boxing／耿 軍 著
——初版，——臺北市，大展，2007〔民 96・11〕
面；21 公分，——（少林傳統功夫漢英對照系列；8）
ISBN 978-957-468-570-7（平裝）

1.拳術 2.中國

528.97 96017580

燕 青 拳

ISBN 978-957-468-570-7

著 者／耿 軍

責任編輯／孔 令 良

發 行 人／蔡 森 明

出 版 者／大展出版社有限公司

社 址／台北市北投區（石牌）致遠一路 2 段 12 巷 1 號

電 話／（02）28236031・28236033・28233123

傳 眞／（02）28272069

郵政劃撥／01669551

網 址／www.dah-jaan.com.tw

E－mail／service@dah-jaan.com.tw

登 記 證／局版臺業字第 2171 號

承 印 者／傳興印刷有限公司

裝 訂／建鑫裝訂有限公司

排 版 者／弘益電腦排版有限公司

授 權 者／北京人民體育出版社

初版 1 刷／2007 年（民 96 年）11 月

定 價／180 元

●本書若有破損、缺頁敬請寄回本社更換●

大展好書　好書大展
品嚐好書　冠群可期